The Road Through Homelessness

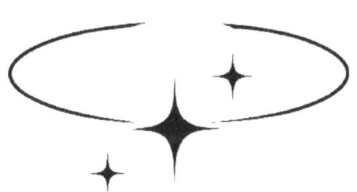

By
Shantel Morris

16 Northolt Rd,
South Harrow, Harrow HA2 0ER,
United Kingdom

Copyright © 2025 Shantel Morris

ISBN (Paperback)
ISBN (Hardback)

All rights reserved

Cover Design by London Book Publisher

No part of this publication may be reproduced, stored in a retrieval system, copied in any form or by any means, electronic, mechanical, photocopying, recording or otherwise transmitted without written permission from the publisher.

You must not circulate this book in any format. Under no circumstances will any blame or legal responsibility be held against the publisher, or author, for any damages, reparation, or monetary loss due to the information contained within this book, either directly or indirectly.

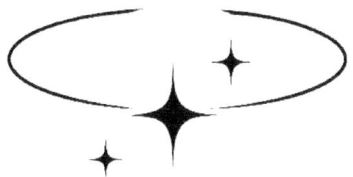

TABLE OF CONTENTS

PREAMBLE	1
PART I: FOUNDATIONS	3
CHAPTER 1: FEARS AND NIGHTMARES	4
CHAPTER 2: MASKS AND SHADOWS	9
CHAPTER 3: LONDON CALLING	14
PART II: LOSS AND DISCOVERY	18
CHAPTER 4: LOSING MUMMY	19
CHAPTER 5: THE WORLD IS YOUR OYSTER	21
CHAPTER 6: ITCHY FEET AND NEW BEGINNINGS	27
PART III: LOVE, LOSS, AND MOTHERHOOD	30
CHAPTER 7: A NEW LIFE - PREGNANCY	31
CHAPTER 8: HOME IS WHERE THE HEART IS	35
CHAPTER 9: CRACKS LIKE FAULT LINES	37
PART IV: HOMELESSNESS AND AWAKENING	42
CHAPTER 10: WE ARE HOMELESS	43
CHAPTER 11: EVICTION DAY	47
CHAPTER 12: FIGHT FOR OUR RIGHTS	50
CHAPTER 13: FOLLOW THE YELLOW BRICK ROAD	56
EPILOGUE: I ONCE WAS LOST BUT NOW I AM FOUND	58

PREAMBLE

This isn't just a book — it's a journey. My journey. The story of who I became **after everything** — after the breakdowns, the breakthroughs, the spiritual awakening, and finally discovering my purpose.

I was chosen. Not because I was perfect, but because I was willing. God, in His infinite grace, sent His angels and His Spirit to guide me through every twist, every dark valley, and every miraculous moment of my life. And in doing so, He revealed my purpose: **to share my truth** and to use my voice to help others find theirs.

This book is **dedicated first and foremost to God Almighty** — the One who never left my side; to the divine purpose that constantly called me home; to the battles that shaped me, and the grace that rebuilt me.

I also dedicate this to my beloved grandparents, **Gladys Morris and Robin Morris**. Their strength, resilience, and deep-rooted wisdom — carved through generations — remind me every day of where I come from and why I must keep going. They, and all our ancestors, are the quiet power running through my veins.

To my beautiful son, Nile, who is my inspiration and who sees the world differently, opening my mind even further.

And to the radiant spirit of a little girl who touched this world so deeply in such a short time — **Ada Bicakci**. Taken from us far too soon on 3rd August 2024, in a tragedy that should never have happened — a child lost to a reckless act, a bus driver under the influence, who stole her future in an instant on the streets of Bexleyheath. But Ada lives on. Ada's brother, **Ata Bicakci**, who was with Ada at the time of the incident and survived... through the selfless love of **Ben Bora Bicakci** and **Nevgul Bicakci**, who turned grief into giving — donating her organs and saving lives. **Her heartbeat goes on @adasheartbeat.** Her light still shines.

We chose the path of hope, faith, and charity!

This book takes you through the journey from trauma to triumph and how you can become the person you were always meant to be.

PART I:
FOUNDATIONS

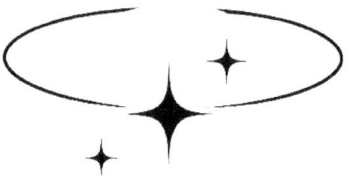

Chapter 1:
Fears and Nightmares

Looking back at photos of myself as a baby, I see a normal, happy child. But one of my earliest memories is fear — specifically, fear of the doctors. The doctor's office had plain beige and brown walls, and the atmosphere in the surgery was gloomy! I picked up on energy very easily and noticed that my mum didn't want to be at the doctor's; you had to be really ill for her to take you there.

"What will they do to me?" I remember asking myself. When the doctor started pulling out equipment from his drawer, I panicked and ran straight out of the room.

I don't remember much from being a younger child, but I do recall glimpses, like when a family friend, who was about seven years old, knocked on the door one day. I'm not sure how, but I answered the door. I was around four years old, and he asked, "Is Stuart (my cousin) coming out to play?"

What happened after that? I don't remember anything. My family remembers that day well. They were responsible for me at that time, but I was eventually found at the park — alone. Where we lived, in those days, there were "Flashers" (men who would expose their bare bodies to young girls). Someone was watching over me, as I was found and made it home safely!

I was born in a small town in Buckinghamshire, England. It was the kind of place where everyone seemed to know each other.

The countryside, where you'd pass farmland on your way from London, was beautiful. There were only a few Black families in the area, so most people knew the Morris name.

My biological mother had me when she was just 18, and my biological father didn't believe I was his daughter, I was told. In Jamaican culture, it wasn't unusual for children to be raised by other family members, especially grandparents.

I was raised by my nan and grandad. My nan was small in stature but big in morals. She was a strict, church-going woman. Gladys, my nan, was the matriarch of the family, even though she was fairly quiet and her presence was still commanding. Gladys's mannerisms and expressions were very funny, especially when she would call us by different names in confusion or when we would be on a car ride: "Oh Robin! (my grandad), wind up the window! You're blowing away my two pieces of hair," in her gentle Jamaican accent.

Mummy was very family-oriented; every birthday was celebrated religiously, and she supported her children by looking after all the grandchildren. She was extremely selfless. After returning home from her shifts as an NHS nurse, she would rustle up something to eat! Mummy's "two piece of rice," as she called it, and was demolished by my cousin and me after we smelt the lovely aroma of fried rice (the edges of the rice pot with leftover gravy).

My grandad stood tall against Gladys with his broad shoulders, and was very quiet, but when he spoke, he had a strong, deep Jamaican accent. I often asked Mummy, "What did he say?" to get a translation so I could communicate with him. My grandad worked hard as he was forced to be a farmer from the age of 12 after his dad died, so his strength was forged under pressure. His feelings and emotions were not necessary for survival. My grandad had the energy of a warrior, which made him seem harsh, but he had a dry sense of humour. He farmed his own fruit and veg in Buckinghamshire. My grandad showed his love through his actions, and I knew he had a kind heart, but when he said

"Shantel," his tone always had depth, regardless of why he was calling. I was fearful of him, as he generally spoke only when he was angry. I was far too scared to get in trouble.

From a young age, I remember feeling a deep sadness, but I learned to hide the sadness behind a smile. When my mum came to visit with my new baby brother and her new partner, I was so happy to hold my brother. After having spent time with my mum, I was confused and upset that she was leaving. I wanted to stay in those moments, but they were always short-lived. When I was in London visiting my mum on school holidays, I really enjoyed the times we spent going to Leicester Square for Baskin-Robbins ice cream sundaes and seeing the bright lights of London.

At times, my relationship with my biological mum felt more like I was her niece than her daughter. I wanted to feel something deeper, physically closer, a genuine bond, but it just wasn't there.

At school, I became the joker, always trying to make people laugh, hoping they'd like me if I could just keep them entertained.

As a child, I always felt different, even though I hung out with the popular and sporty kids. In middle school—around eight years old—I started receiving extra support from a teacher. It was meant to help, but it only made me feel more different and uncomfortable. I already had low self-esteem, and I didn't get the kind of emotional reassurance I needed growing up at home.

So I did what I had learned to do: I masked it. I wore my smile like armour. And to most people, that's all they ever saw—my smile. I had perfected it.

I remember the school nurse weighing me and telling me I was "big-boned." At that age, those words stuck with me more than anyone realised.

My broad shoulders and athletic build made me self-conscious. I felt I looked masculine, even though I adapted well to sports.

Sports were my outlet, and as I grew, netball became a light. I was competitive and good at it.

In our family, emotional support just wasn't a thing. Jamaican children were traditionally expected to be "seen and not heard." There were no hugs or "I love yous," which was tough for someone like me, already struggling with feelings of abandonment. My biological mother left to work in London when I was about three, and my grandparents—Mummy and Daddy—raised me. I didn't understand why, so I eventually assumed there was something wrong with me.

Emotions... feelings were not necessary or wanted in our family, and as an emotional child, I really struggled. If I was hurt and crying, naturally I would seek help from my nan. She would say, "Get the Dettol."

When I was scared at night, I would go to my nan and ask, "Can I sleep with you?" I was allowed. "Ok," she said.

I enjoyed the safety of being squashed between my nan and grandad. I felt safe between them, like no one could hurt me there. But finding out what my worries were was not the done thing in our culture, so they remained constantly boiling like lava, waiting to erupt like a volcano. I was slowly, indirectly being desensitised by what someone would say or do. Being soft or sensitive was considered a weakness.

"Don't kiss the baby, Shantel," I was told. I didn't understand why, because I had such a natural affection for babies.

Mummy worked as an NHS nurse, and Daddy worked in a factory. They were busy raising my aunt, uncle, my cousin, and me after their three eldest daughters had left. When Daddy was made redundant due to discrimination in his forties, he couldn't find more work. We didn't have much, but we made do. Our upbringing was strict and traditional—church every Sunday, and it was compulsory to attend Sunday school as it was passed down through generations. Respect for elders was paramount.

My cousin, aunts, and uncle were like siblings to me. My younger cousins felt like my babies, and I adored them, often saying to my aunts, "Can I feed them?" or after a nap, "I'll pick him up."

When I was about ten years old, I always felt anxious and scared to ask questions. In-depth conversations were not encouraged at home, and I often felt very alone and had no one to talk to. I wanted help but did not know who would listen.

I was scared of my room — convinced someone was in there if I was alone upstairs. I had nightmares, and I was scared to go to sleep one night after I saw an advert on the TV about Dracula. I was so scared I slept with the light on and had the cover right over my head, thinking he was coming for me. Then, I started to feel what felt like little spiders running down my face. I shot out of bed and ran downstairs.

Strange nightmares about tidal waves coming out of nowhere and our home being washed away, nightmares about people chasing me... I could just about get away, slightly levitating off the ground. My aunts and uncle would say occasionally in the mornings, "You were talking in your sleep again last night," or, "Don't you remember you came downstairs last night?" referring to my sleepwalking. As an 11-year-old, I felt buried in fear, sorrow, and confusion.

Our family had strong personalities, and disputes often led to silence and avoidance. No one talked things out. I learned to mimic this passive-aggressive behaviour.

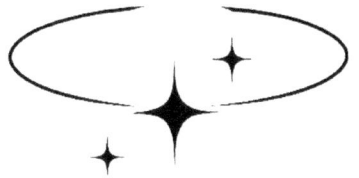

CHAPTER 2:
MASKS AND SHADOWS

In secondary school, my netball team and I played so well together that we became notorious in our town. We would play every Saturday with friends and elders, and I briefly played for the county. I was also good at sprinting and was regularly put forward for District sports competitions. Competition and playing sports made me feel something other than sadness. It was exhilarating and taught me to fight... to push through to win and get that feeling of happiness. The team were my friends; we spent so much time together. I felt like I belonged.

At school, I would often get distracted from doing my work. "Urrrrgh, Shantel," the teacher would call my name in a dissenting tone after I'd been talking to my friends.

I craved recognition — the adrenaline of being noticed for doing something well. Sometimes, I'd indirectly break the rules to impress my friends. I wasn't allowed out much. "It's not good to hang out on the street!" my mum would say in her firm Jamaican accent. If Gladys was really mad, we'd get the infamous "side-eye", and she'd kiss her teeth then flick her head in the other direction.

My once-a-week call on a Friday with my biological mother was difficult. I would sit twirling the long, curly cord of the landline phone in the hallway, saying "they never let me out", referring to my grandparents.

Even though I grew up in what felt like a loveless environment, I had so much love to give. I knew, as an adult, I wanted to work with children or become a hairdresser — something that would allow me to care for others. I remember my amazing PE teacher, Mrs King, asking me once, "What do you want to be when you're older?" When I told her, she looked at me and said, "You could do so much more." That stayed with me and made me think, what did she mean?

Mrs Smith was kind and brilliant at teaching maths, and I connected with her energy, which made learning maths enjoyable. Mr Devlin would let us have tea and biscuits during wet play. Those little things meant so much more than they probably knew, but I felt that these teachers saw me and told me I had potential. Their actions supported me, which gave me such comfort.

I spent a lot of time at home as a child, in my room, feeling low. Netball gave me a sense of purpose, something to hold on to, but most of the time, by the time I reached secondary school, my depression had worsened. I felt everything more deeply than others seemed to. I was the sensitive one — the "black sheep" of the family. I felt ugly and confused, still trying to make sense of why I was being raised by my grandparents instead of my parents.

The day I was confirmed in Church (a ceremony to confirm my commitment to God) was horrible. It felt like everyone was coming for the ceremony but not really coming for me. It overwhelmed me. "I do not want to be confirmed," I told my mother. In my mind, what I really wanted was to be heard and to be asked how I felt! She said, "Once you do this, you won't have to go to church anymore."

My depression led to two suicide attempts; I just couldn't take it... the feelings were drowning me. I rarely saw my biological mother — just birthdays or Christmases, with a weekly phone call. At 12, my mum asked if I wanted to live with her in London, but I said no. I didn't want to leave my netball or my friends, and that was all I had. London felt too far, too big, too unfamiliar.

A few months later, I started taking risks. I didn't understand the danger. I remember one time vividly. My friend and I ended up at the house of a boy from school I liked. We went inside. His older cousin was there. Suddenly, the cousin grabbed me and wrestled me to the ground. My friend was pushed outside by the boy, who now held my legs down. The cousin tried to assault me, but I fought with all my strength. My friend was banging on the window, trying to help. When I heard the cousin say, "Take her trousers off," I knew that my body was going to be exposed. My trousers were lowered by the boy, while the top half of my body was pinned down. I thought, he was my school friend, how could he be doing this? Something shifted in him — he hesitated — and that gave me the chance to push his cousin off and run. I escaped, half-dressed and shaken. I never told anyone. I just wanted to forget.

At 15, while on holiday in Jamaica, I disappeared with a man I had just met, putting myself in dangerous situations just for the thrill. I loved the excitement, the adrenaline.

Secondary school had its highs and lows. I enjoyed sports and kept distracted. There were name-calling moments — "big head" and "gorilla" — from a couple of the boys, but overall, I did not take any notice of them. They only confirmed that I was ugly. I had decided at an early age that I enjoyed being creative with hair. I loved playing with my friends' hair, so it was a natural progression after school to go to college. It was strange leaving school, but the excitement of something new and a new environment outweighed the fact I might miss some friends. I started trying new styles while I was at college, but my self-esteem was still very low. I was clearly different — the "black girl". I felt like a grown-up at college. All of these experiences distracted me from the black fog; the external energies and interests were keeping me busy. I was given an apprenticeship at a salon and quickly took to a part-time work life where I earned my own money, which I quickly spent on a new outfit every other week to go out to the clubs at the weekend. Boys always seemed interested in my friends, and I craved to have that attention. I would wear low-cut tops and tight clothes, thinking it would make me more attractive. I hoped that one day someone would choose me.

Whilst studying, I accidentally met my biological dad's wife as I was styling her daughter's (my step-sister's) hair. It was such a strange feeling. I was 18 and had never met my dad or anyone on his side of the family. We got on so well, and she invited me over to meet the rest of the family. I was very curious and hoped that he would accept me with open arms, telling me, "I've missed you," but I was met with a strange energy, as if he was not interested. I noticed the resemblance between my dad and me, but internally I knew I was my own person. I was so happy to meet the rest of the family – the girls... two step-sisters and three half-sisters. But something felt off with my dad. I couldn't put my finger on it; not only was he unresponsive towards me, but the girls seemed very quiet and sad. About a month later, I had an urgent call from my stepmother, who said I had to come over. The news was horrific... my biological dad was abusing my step-sister, who was twelve. My stepmother and I were both in tears, and that was the last day we spoke. I could not handle it... I brushed it under the carpet, but deep down inside, I wondered if I was like that as he was my dad. I thought about it for a few days. *Would the girls hate me?* Maybe I should stay away. The guilt on his behalf cut me deeply, and I felt so bad for my step-sister, who had suffered so badly, and for my stepmother.

I drowned my feelings in nightlife, going to clubs and drinking. One night we went to a club... it was so hot, dark, and smoky (in the days when you could still smoke in clubs in the UK and leave a club smelling like an ashtray, with your hair all frizzy from the heat after spending hours straightening it). In the corner, I saw this guy – tall, dark, and handsome. I knew his friend and asked, "Who's your friend?" He replied, "Talk to him," so I did. "What's your name?" He replied, "Rodney." We started talking. I felt so happy. I smiled so much, I had a jaw ache. I could not contain my excitement, and I fancied him so much. This was the first time in my life that I really felt wanted, and he was interested in me – me!!

Our conversation led to a long-distance relationship at first, for about a year. We would talk to each other every day for hours. I would visit him, and he would visit me. My grandparents were vexed when I started coming home late or calling, saying I missed the last train. When my granddad saw the phone bill, he said, "Shantel, you're not using the phone anymore." I felt that he was stopping me from seeing Rodney and left the room crying. On the way to my bedroom, Mummy stopped me and hugged me. I was in shock... a hug, something I had always wanted, and I held on to it regardless of the unusual feeling. It meant so much to me to be consoled when I was upset. From that moment on, I had to resort to payphones on the street to call Rodney.

I could not stop seeing Rodney in London because he made me happy, but I still tried to follow Daddy's house rules at home. I slipped up again, missing the train, and Daddy was furious, saying, "You treat this place like a hotel," followed by, "Get out!!"

I did not know what to do. I went upstairs crying and packing a bag. Mummy quickly followed.

"What are you doing?" she said.

"I'm going," I replied.

"Where?" she asked.

I had no idea, but I knew that I was likely to make more mistakes.

Chapter 3: London Calling

Eventually, I moved to London to live with Rodney. We lived in a one-bedroom flat in a block of flats in East London, and the flat was nice. At first, it was great living with Rodney. My boyfriend was very streetwise, and he made me laugh... I was very trusting — some might say gullible. I believed people were kind and honest, and all I wanted was to be liked. I worked in an exclusive location and often saw celebrities. In fact, I served Robbie Williams in the shop. These exciting moments and vibrant areas gave me short-lived contentment and occasional happy feelings.

But unfortunately, the reality of living in a big city hit me. There were a few occasions that made me realise it wasn't safe where we lived.

On a couple of occasions, I'd come home from work and say to Rodney, "The front door is broken again." We lived on a main road, and it disturbed me that anyone could walk into the main door of the building. This was definitely the case, as a few months later, I saw needles on the floor outside our door, near our neighbour's flat. I told Rodney, and he replied, "He's a druggie."

There was a lot of respect and admiration when people heard I worked in Central London. On the other hand, deep down, I had for a longing to belong, to be whole, to be accepted. Even my boyfriend, who was so caring, couldn't fix the deep wounds I had inside or stop the black fog. I quickly realised I wasn't in a small town outside of London anymore, and not everyone was as honest as I had thought.

But the mask I wore began to crack. The stress at work and the tension at home became overwhelming; I felt like it was coming from both sides. Rodney and I argued about silly things. "We need a new sofa; it's falling apart," I said. He replied, "It's fine." A month later, he had a new computer. I started feeling suicidal again; I couldn't handle the constant arguments between us. It was so draining. Deep down, I was still incredibly lonely. I avoided my thoughts, bottled up my feelings, and they would sometimes erupt like a volcano. I wasn't an angry person, but my inner child was deeply hurt and crying out for attention.

I just couldn't hold it together anymore; I was at a point where I was thinking, "Why am I here?" I visited the doctor because I needed help. I entered the room and sat down, and she said, "I have a trainee with me today." I thought, "It's hard enough opening up to the doctor, let alone to two people." Then the doctor said, "What can I help you with?" My eyes immediately started to fill with tears. I said, "I... I don't know," my lip turned down, and the tears started streaming down. "I don't know what's wrong." I broke down in the doctor's office. The doctor could see I was struggling to speak and started to ask me questions to understand how I was feeling and why. She offered antidepressants, but I didn't take them after speaking to my biological mother, who advised me not to — mental health was a cultural taboo in our culture, and medication was a no-go. In Jamaican culture, you just get on with life, regardless of what happens. There's no point in feeling or crying about it. How bad can it be if you're not working on the plantation as a slave? Everyone had secrets or stories. There was a lot of talk about Prozac making you numb, that it could really make you mad or fat! Strength is power in Jamaican culture, whether physical or mental, and to say you're not mentally strong is definitely seen as a weakness — one that someone could use against you.

Even with a big family, I didn't feel understood, and explaining my feelings would often be met with judgemental, unhelpful comments.

Everyone was busy with their own lives, and the differences between Rodney and me became clear with the constant arguments. Just before our relationship ended, we were burglarised. When I got home, the door was visibly forced open, and a lot of sentimental jewellery was taken. The fact that someone could so easily get into my home caused me a lot of anxiety. I had to leave Rodney, but doing so easily led me back into risky behaviours and the need to feel wanted. It was like I was trying to fix the depression and self-medicate, without realising I was doing it.

I worked as a makeup artist in a London department store, and it was a visual delight seeing the transformations. Our makeup studio was stunning, with full-length mirrors, pale wood flooring, and wardrobes. Everything to the eye was externally pleasing, and I tried to distract myself by going out to different clubs.

I had highs from the energy of dancing in clubs; I loved to dance—and dance with boys, especially. It made me feel wanted, like I had achieved something. After dancing with a guy and talking to someone I really liked, he said, "Can I have your number?" I was so happy; my face lit up. I'd go home and wait eagerly for the phone call. Once he called me once, I took it into my own hands to call back whenever I wanted. This was a cry for love and to feel needed. I would often practise this "I am available" routine with boys and noticed that they generally disappeared within days.

One day, a man pulled over while I was walking and asked for my number. I felt seen. We spoke on the phone, and he offered to pick me up later. He seemed nice and said we could talk more comfortably at his place. I was 21—young, naïve. I agreed. That evening, he picked me up and drove about 20 minutes to a council estate. I thought we would go out. Inside, he guided me to a small flat. He started kissing me, then tried to remove my trousers. I said, "No." He stopped—briefly—then tried again. I said, "No" again. This time, he held my wrists above my head. I panicked and thought, "I'm in trouble." My resistance didn't stop him. After it was over, he took me home. I only told the sexual health clinic. I pushed it to the back of my mind, with all the other buried pain. I continued working in skincare and sales. Outwardly, my life looked like that of any 22-year-old—clubs, work, friends—but inside, I was lonely and lost.

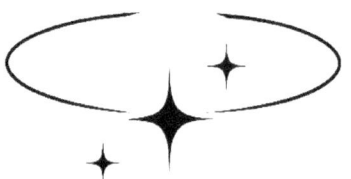

PART II:
LOSS AND DISCOVERY

CHAPTER 4:
LOSING MUMMY

One day, I looked at my mum and realised that she had lost a lot of weight, so I said to her, "Mum, you've lost weight," and quickly followed with, "You need to go to the doctor." Something told me that she wasn't well.

Mummy would never go to the doctor, and unless we were really ill — on the floor — we would never be taken to the doctor either. I suppose she knew she wasn't well but hid it. She did go to the doctor in February 2013, and mum was diagnosed with cancer, but it had spread so much that the doctors couldn't determine where the cancer had originated. Mum suffered over the next few months, unable to eat and screaming in the night in a lot of pain. Eventually, they said that the cancer had spread to her hip, and she would need a hip replacement.

After mum's hip replacement, she fell into a coma. At this point, I prayed that she would die, as she was suffering so much. I had never seen my mum sick, let alone go through all this pain, as she was such a strong woman who never complained. After witnessing my mum having a seizure, it was incredibly difficult. A couple of days after a scan, the doctors said, "The cancer has spread to her brain."

Everyone knew she was in so much pain, and it was so hard to see her like that, but the general feeling among the family was that she had suffered enough. After seeing mum have a seizure, I knew her time was nearing an end, and a few nights later, I prayed to God to relieve her from her suffering. My mum passed away in June 2013; it was a blessing, but also incredibly hard, as she was the matriarch of the family.

My mum was small in stature but a force to be reckoned with. She didn't take any prisoners; just one firm look from her would send fear down your spine. On the other hand, she had such a laugh and a special smile. She would give you everything she could to help anyone. My mum loved children and helped all of her children by looking after her grandchildren when needed. Mum did a lot, especially the fact that she allowed my biological mother to continue living her life without having the full-time responsibility of a child.

After my mum's funeral, I realised that life would be very different, and the person I had called mum for twenty-three years was truly gone. Months after mum passed, there was an altercation within the family. I couldn't take it and left the house in tears.

Part of me felt like I was running away from the situation, from the grief, and the other part saw this as an opportunity to escape the massive change that was taking place in the family. I was good at running from confrontation — it made me so anxious after seeing family arguments in the past. I had previously witnessed my aunts and uncle having extremes of jokes, followed by years of not speaking to each other. I didn't realise at the time, but I had done the same thing after I left my aunt's house following an altercation.

So many different feelings ran through my head after mum's death — flashbacks of her having seizures after the cancer spread to her brain, and her falling into a coma. "How could it happen to her, such a kind woman?"

There was part of me that wanted to honour my mum, her legacy of kindness, care, and family.

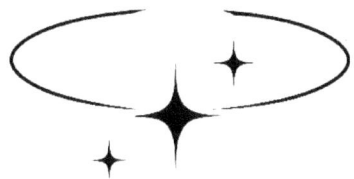

Chapter 5:
The World is Your Oyster

Working in what I initially thought were London's grand and glamorous department stores eventually became mundane, and I wanted more from life. I spoke to a lady on the cosmetics floor who said she had worked on a cruise ship before, and I was in shock!

She said, "I went to Singapore."

I replied, "What's that? Where's that?"

I had never heard of half of the places she mentioned! She then spoke about how, as merchandise staff, you could go on excursions when you got off the ship. I didn't even know what that was, and she explained in more detail. My eyes grew bigger and bigger. I was like a five-year-old asking multiple questions. I was fascinated by the idea of something different and somewhere different… "Maybe I can find what I am looking for out there," even though I didn't really know what I was looking for!

Shortly after my mum passed away, I took a leap of faith. I got a job working on a cruise ship. I packed my bags as I had successfully found a job working as a merchandise assistant on a cruise ship in the Mediterranean. I had no real expectations, and when I got off the plane in Majorca, the new location instantly gave me a feeling of joy. We worked hard, as we didn't get a day off and worked long hours, but the experience was unforgettable. I saw so many beautiful places, like Barcelona, Naples (with its crazy moped a.k.a. Vespa drivers), the scenic Toulon, and Malta.

Being in Italy felt like I was on a pilgrimage, visiting sights like the Sistine Chapel and the Vatican. The pure beauty of the architecture alone was remarkable, but the atmosphere was incomparable. The picturesque Portofino was stunning with its little coloured townhouses and a variety of boats/yachts.

As we cruised down the Strait of Sardinia in the early evening, with the sunset just having gone down, we could see the lights of the coast highlighting the houses on one side, and on the other side, a dark, rugged mountain slope. As we approached closer, one side of the mountain had a few houses highlighted by lights, while the other side was a vibrant reddish/orange. It was the active volcano Stromboli – I can still smell the sulphur. Seeing the power of Mother Nature in person was mind-blowing! The free-roaming monkeys in Gibraltar were fascinating. One lady tried to stroke a baby monkey, and the mother fly-kicked her.

It was mentally and emotionally challenging working on the cruise ship as I was grieving, but also, it was my first time away from the UK for more than two weeks. I was a small-town girl who had moved to London at nineteen and was now enjoying the breathtaking views of the sea. This gave me a sense of calm and joy, which was such a spiritual experience. The way the ship moved through the still waters made me feel like time had stood still. It was indirect meditation and gave me so much inner peace.

Seeing different parts of the world made me realise that there is a vast world out there with different cultures and people. I was fascinated by the number of different people working on the cruise ship, speaking various languages.

About a month after I started working on the cruise, I clearly heard my mum's voice say "Shantel" while I was about to sleep one night on the ship.

I leapt from my bed, looking around. I wanted to see her, and her voice brought me comfort. I questioned myself, wondering if it had really happened, but deep down inside, I knew it was her.

After five months, I was homesick and very tired. I wanted to stay on the cruise ship for the crossing to Brazil and complete another season, but I just couldn't keep up with the 12-hour days and only a few hours off here and there. When I returned to the UK, I had nowhere to stay. As always, my uncle stepped in for me and let me stay at his place. He always felt more like an older brother, someone who's consistently looked out for me.

Shortly after I returned home, I saw an outline of my mum in the very early hours of the morning while staying at my uncle's studio flat. My uncle had given up his bed for me while he slept on the sofa. Something woke me up, and it was dark outside, but the streetlights always slightly lit the room. As I briefly sat up in bed, looking out past the sofa to the window, I briefly saw a silhouette of her leaning over him, and then it disappeared. I couldn't believe my eyes, blinking several times and wondering if I was dreaming. But the room and bed were too real, with too much detail, for it not to be real.

I always knew that there was a spiritual side to my grandparents, as they spoke about dreams on rare occasions, but only if they were asked about it. They had a gift. After I saw my mummy, I told my granddad. I asked him if he had seen her too, and my granddad said, "Yes!"

My granddad would mumble in his sleep regularly, so loud that I could hear him in the next room.

"Who were you talking to?" I said the next day.

He replied, "Your grandmother."

I made the decision to go back to the UK because I thought I was missing out, but I quickly realised that I needed more and wanted to travel more.

A year later, I applied to work in Egypt as a holiday rep and ended up staying there for almost two years. I loved Egypt and the Egyptian people, and I was able to see so much. I saw the busy city of Cairo, the wonder of the pyramids, and the Valley of the Kings in Luxor. The contrast of the yellow mountains against the blue sea was mesmerising.

At one point, I was based in Egypt near the Israeli border, so I was able to visit Jerusalem. It had such an indescribable feeling, knowing that I was walking in the steps of Jesus was such a spiritual experience.

Standing on top of Masada Mountain, I went to Jordan to see Petra.

Facing my fears has always been something I needed and wanted to do. Being in Egypt, I had the opportunity to do so. I heard about a "try dive," where an experienced diver would hold you, so I signed up. As I got the scuba gear, my anxiety built, my heart was beating fast, and excitement came in waves.

As we entered the water, the diver asked, "Are you ready?"

I said, "No," with a smile, and followed with a "Yes." As we descended into the water, I started to breathe through the regulator. He said, "Slow breaths." It was easier said than done when I was petrified and did the complete opposite. I eventually slightly slowed down my breathing, and we started to descend into the clear waters. Immediately, the diver pointed out the coral, and my eyes popped out of my head. The coral and the fish looked unreal. I couldn't believe it – the colours were so bold! I felt so light and free in the water; I completely forgot I was attached to the diver. I needed more of this feeling. Shortly after, I started an open water PADI course.

This experience made me realise how much fear had held me back for so long, especially after the experiences I had as a child in the pool. The water going up my nose made it feel horribly fizzy, and I almost drowned, which put me off swimming altogether. I loved snorkelling in the sea, exploring the corals with the array of fish and vibrant colours. It was freeing, flowing with the water as the sun shone on the surface, highlighting and reflecting light on the sea.

Living in Egypt, I was near Mount Sinai. Climbing Mount Sinai (a.k.a. Moses Mountain) was a tribute to my mum. I wanted to do it for her. We walked up the rugged mountain at 3am so we could reach the top for sunrise at 6am. It was exhausting getting to the top, but seeing the sunrise light up the mountainous desert landscape was breathtaking… if there was any breath left after the three-hour trek! But I felt spiritually closer to God and my mum after the spectacular experience.

Coming down was ten times harder than going up, as now the sun was up, and I could see how high up I was. I froze several times, shaking in fear. Everyone was passing me. This was the point where I had to find the strength to face my fear of heights.

Living and working in Egypt taught me to slow down and appreciate the experiences of exploring the ancient land — the sights, the peace — but I still felt something inside was missing! I felt like maybe I was becoming an adrenaline junkie, always wanting more experiences, as they were the only things that made me feel alive and excited about living. They brought light and fun to my life.

Regardless of all the people and all my experiences, I still felt lonely, plus that something was missing. My feelings were pushed deep down inside, and I kept busy to avoid addressing the issues.

During my time in Egypt, I also realised that I love experiencing hotels, the grandeur, the luxury. I visited many hotels as part of my job, taking care of the resort guests from the UK. I loved visiting the five-star Renaissance Hotel. The interior was furnished with ornate golden chairs and pearly white walls, and the sea view from the circular lobby was dazzling, so opulent. I felt at home in these surroundings. This felt somehow like I had experienced this luxury before. I would be invited to enjoy breakfast, and the waffles would melt in your mouth. The flavours, while looking out onto the contrasting blues of the sea, created bi-sensory experiences at once, filling me with joy, peace, and comfort... I took a deep breath and sighed with pleasure. The external pleasures temporarily satisfied me.

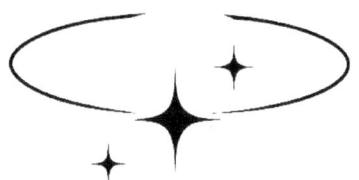

CHAPTER 6:
ITCHY FEET AND NEW BEGINNINGS

Travelling had always been a passion of mine, and I knew I wanted to continue. I landed a job as an adventure guide (a sort of travel concierge for tourists/guest experiences job) for Adventures by Disney. As part of our training, we experienced Disney World and its parks! I was pleasantly surprised—it turned out to be the best experience. Each park was enormous. It was easy to get lost, but I had a group of friends, and we explored the parks together. The rides were incredible, and we even ran across one of the parks to catch our booking for the Cirque du Soleil show. These were truly "WOW" experiences!

When I co-guided trips with guests from London to Paris, it felt like luxury – we stayed in 5-star hotels like the Renaissance, enjoyed first-class sightseeing, travelled in First Class on the Eurostar, and attended Disney theatre productions. We had Fast Track access to the Eiffel Tower. I even met Joey from NSYNC and took care of his family. On one of our special trips, we were informed that we would be guiding the CEO of Disney and his family on an Adventures by Disney tour. I was tasked with collecting Bob Iger near the Louvre in Paris. As I met him and his son at the car, we began walking through the **Tuileries Garden** towards the Louvre for a VIP tour. Just then, a bird flew overhead and pooped on his head.

Bob noticed and said to his son, handing him a tissue, "Help me get this off, please." His son, laughing, replied, "No." I said, "Let me help."

The job was seasonal, and after it finished, I was offered a contract to work on the Disney Wonder cruise ship for the winter season, which travelled from Disney Island to the Bahamas and Florida. I loved working with Disney; the energy of the characters was amazing, and I met people from all over the world. However, it was hard work, though a great experience. I eventually realised I needed to come back to the "real world," so I secured a job as a sales representative for a UK sightseeing company. I met some wonderful people, both among the company staff and concierge teams at hotels.

I loved visiting London's 5-star hotels, such as the Savoy and the Ritz. They exuded luxury, from their scents to the glittering colours and décor. Doors opened for me, and I was treated with respect and a smile, with no judgement—only acceptance. I had regular meetings and celebrated at gala dinners in evening gowns, enjoying champagne, caviar, and other delights. My work required attending late-night networking events every month, as building strong relationships with hotels was a key part of the role. Work became a huge part of my life.

Everything seemed to be going well, and I had saved enough money to buy my first home, with a loan from my uncle. When I finally got the keys to my own home, it felt surreal. I had made it. All of my hard work since I was a teenager had led to this moment. Coming from a family who lived in a council house, where we shared a small chicken between five people, and now having a flat completely refurbished—I was so happy to finally own my home after a decade of private renting. It was such an achievement for me. No more paying someone else's rent, no more living in tiny studio flats, and no more sharing flats with people who didn't clean the bath!

As I stood in the lavish Dorchester Hotel in London, wearing an elegant evening gown and sipping a cocktail, I was the picture of success. I was with my Managing Director and a team member, waiting for the rest of my team to arrive. This was the annual Gala Dinner event, and I was living my best life! I felt seen at these events when our partners and clients saw me; they were happy to see me. I had formed strong relationships with a select few. I stood out! The vibrant energy of the room matched my own—the life and soul of the party, a confident woman who always spoke her mind.

I thrived on laughter, dancing, and the exhilaration of new experiences. Afternoon teas and cocktails at luxurious hotels had become a monthly tradition, and indulging in the finer things had become my norm. I loved every minute of it! Yet, part of me wondered if this was real or just a façade—were we all pretending to be happy and that everything was fine, while beneath the surface, cracks were beginning to show?

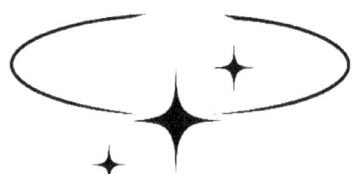

PART III:
LOVE, LOSS, AND MOTHERHOOD

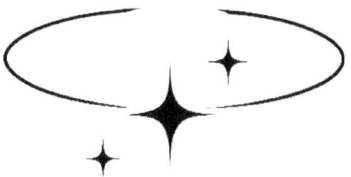

CHAPTER 7:
A NEW LIFE - PREGNANCY

I was walking through the park on my way to the gym and saw a man working out. I couldn't help but look at him, though I tried not to let him notice that I had seen him. As I made my way across the park, I could see him out of the corner of my eye approaching me. I didn't know what to do with myself. There was a mix of excitement and anxiety. He started to walk directly towards me and said, "Hi... my name is Mr."

From that moment, it felt like a whirlwind romance—or at least, that's what I thought. We were together constantly, and after a few days, I was staying at his house.

On our first date, Mr told me, "I don't eat pork," while we were looking at the menu. He seemed disgusted by it, especially when I wanted to order it, saying, "Please don't get that." For some reason, I wanted to please him and didn't order it. I found myself in a position where I started avoiding pork altogether to keep him happy.

After a month, we went on holiday together to Spain, and that was when I saw a darker side of Mr We were at a restaurant ordering food, and he told me to pick something for him. I ordered paella and told the waitress, "No pork." The waitress brought the dish out, and he raised his voice, "What's that, pork?" Out of the corner of my eye, I could see everyone looking at us. The waitress seemed confused and scared as she didn't speak much English.

I said, "It's okay... I'll eat it," as I felt so bad for the way he spoke to the waitress. He replied, "No, you won't," and stormed off. I was embarrassed and scared! He apologised later that night, reminding me of his strong dislike for pork and how bad it was. We continued with the holiday, but that was the first time I saw his anger and control. It wasn't the last, though. Mr could go from calm to furious in seconds. At times, he seemed like Dr Jekyll and Mr Hyde, but generally, he appeared fine.

When we returned to the UK, things seemed to be going well apart from his occasional flare-ups. I thought, "If I didn't have him, what would I have?" I suggested that we move into the flat I had bought, rather than have two separate places. He agreed and moved in after two months. I loved him; I thought I could help him, change him even, and hoped we would work.

Mr moved in with me, but within the first month, I saw a very dark side to him. His anger could flare up over the smallest things. At first, I felt sorry for him, as he would apologise profusely hours after his outbursts, often in a depression-like state. We had many arguments in the coming months.

After six years working for a sightseeing company, I became pregnant after six months with my boyfriend at the time. I was happy, but my son was unplanned, and there were already serious doubts about my relationship with my boyfriend. Mr said that he didn't feel like our home was his place. He often said, "It's YOUR flat!" Well, it was my flat that I had worked hard to achieve, but I thought a new home might help by giving him and Nile the space they needed. My mother advised me that a bigger home might ease the tension in our one-bedroom flat — the place where arguments over finances, childcare, and respect were all too common.

The doctors told me my pregnancy was high-risk, as I had high blood pressure and fibroids. I was frequently in the hospital for routine check-ups but was assured that my fibroids would not affect my ability to deliver. During the pregnancy, the fibroids grew rapidly with Nile and would wake me up at night in agony, which was very scary. I was booked for a scheduled labour, as the doctors wanted to induce me after 38 weeks due to the high-risk nature of the pregnancy.

On the day of my induction, I had two attempts to bring on labour, but neither worked and only negatively affected Nile's heartbeat. I knew something was wrong when the doctors couldn't break my waters and when the midwife could no longer hear Nile's heartbeat. The decision was made quickly that I needed a general anaesthetic, and Nile had to be delivered immediately. When I came around from the anaesthetic, the midwife said, "Look at your baby," but I was in so much pain. I think I passed out again, and when I woke up, I was in intensive care. The nurse told me that Nile was with his dad, and I had lost three pints of blood.

I felt so sick that I didn't fully understand what had happened. I drifted off to sleep again, and when I woke up, I was on a ward with Nile in his cot next to me. Mr was sitting beside me, saying, "I was so scared, I thought you had gone, Shan." He also told me, "Nile cried so much when they brought him out to me from surgery." Mr said he took care of Nile completely as I couldn't move, and I didn't have breast milk due to the blood loss. I had wire stitching in my stomach and hadn't got my pain under control properly, plus I was still drowsy.

Mr said he was going to go home to get some sleep and have a shower, as my uncle had come to visit. But when I fell asleep again, I woke up to find Mr angry that I was alone. I wasn't sure what had happened. I definitely felt that Nile and I were protected by God, and that we had a purpose.

After five days in hospital recovering, I returned home and really struggled with the pain and getting to grips with Nile. When Mr went back to work, I became very anxious. I was scared to leave Nile for anything, even to have a shower, so I didn't, until Mr came home. I lived on coffee and biscuits, feeling depressed and lonely. Mr and I argued constantly; he wanted to circumcise Nile, and he didn't want Nile eating pork.

After Nile was born, I was struggling mentally and really needed support, but I didn't feel like I was getting it. What made it worse was that my biological mother lived just ten minutes away. I found myself hoping again that she would "step up," but it didn't happen. I told my biological mother about how I felt and she kept saying things like, "It's because you live in a small space that you're not getting on," and after a while, I started to wonder—was that really the reason? Could living in a one-bedroom flat be the cause of all our problems? Was the space too tight for all the emotions, pressures, and expectations?

I also had to return to work to afford our life, so I started a conversation with Mr.

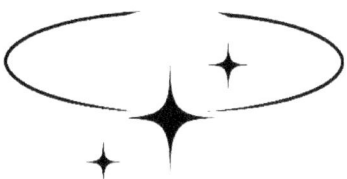

Chapter 8:
Home is Where the Heart is

Mr and I agreed on how we would manage the bills, childcare arrangements, and the upkeep of the home. However, when it came to the official documents to buy a new home, even though Mr did not financially contribute to the deposit or the home improvements, he persuaded me that he would repay me. So, I added his name to the deeds of the house.

In 2015, hoping to keep the family together, I sold my flat and took a massive risk by investing all the profit into moving to a bigger house in a quieter neighbourhood. We moved into a beautiful three-bedroom house with a garden—a space I had worked so hard to provide. I came from a background where a single chicken was shared between six people, and I had sacrificed so much to create this new life.

I returned to work after my maternity leave. We needed the money to pay the mortgage and nursery fees.

Business As Usual

At first, going back to work felt refreshing. It gave me some structure again and a sense of independence. But it didn't take long before I realised that I couldn't keep up with the networking demands of my job in sales. Being a full-time working mum was tough enough—but doing it without proper childcare support made it nearly impossible. My managing director at the time was incredibly supportive and helped me balance things. However, after she left, work became much more challenging. The understanding and flexibility I had enjoyed disappeared, which added to the weight of everything else I was already carrying.

About a year later, I filed a complaint about an uncomfortable incident at work. Mentally, the situation was exhausting, and I felt completely disrespected, as though I was causing trouble for no reason. I had some of the best experiences of my life with this company, but it became clear to me that it was time to leave after I spoke my truth. The situation made me feel like the black sheep again, as grievances were not addressed in the way I felt they should have been. I have always had a strong sense of justice and did not want anyone else to endure what I had gone through, so I fought as hard as I could to stand up for what was right.

This experience took me back to my childhood feelings of unworthiness, and mostly to the realisation that I couldn't speak up or express my truth. I couldn't sleep; it was constantly on my mind. My doctor diagnosed me with anxiety and depression, and I was prescribed antidepressants.

Some might say it was a "David and Goliath" situation, standing up to a large company on my own. After a long battle, I left the company and tried to move on from it.

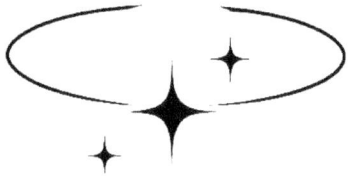

CHAPTER 9: CRACKS LIKE FAULT LINES

After this situation, the cracks in my relationship with my son's dad worsened, and I no longer felt supported by him while I was going through my grief.

One day, we sat down, and I said, "I can't do this anymore," referring to our relationship, and he responded, "I know, but I'll change."

He begged me to try again, and I wanted to believe him because I didn't want Nile to grow up in a single-parent household. Mr and I attended couples counselling, and during the first session, the therapist gently started fact-finding. Mr would always introduce himself with a handshake, a smile, and his name. He consistently presented himself as charming, chatty, and reasonable. When he went to a party, he had to wear brand-new clothes, and his children also had to be dressed in new clothes.

In the second counselling session, it was clear that the counsellor tried to delve deeper and address the issues related to his controlling tendencies, but Mr seemed to shut down. He just could not see it. No matter how much we discussed it, nothing changed. I couldn't keep paying for counselling sessions!

Six months later, I sat down with him again, trying to persuade him that our relationship wasn't working. "Let's have a break," I suggested, but he refused, saying, "It's all in your head."

Another year passed, and the arguments were exactly the same. We slept in separate rooms and barely spoke to each other. He was hardly ever home to care for Nile, and when he was home, he was always sleeping. Unfortunately, I didn't feel like I could talk to my family for support because, growing up, we never discussed our problems.

I felt so alone, especially as my biological mother felt that contact once a week over the phone was enough. I asked her multiple times if she could have Nile for a weekend. She would say she was busy or that "Mr would look after him."

It was getting worse as he became angrier, even in front of Nile. No amount of extra space could mask the growing strain between us, and the arguments continued. I went above and beyond to support us, working long hours and looking after our son with very little help. Once again, I felt sorry for him and thought, "Maybe I can fix him." So, I organised another counselling session, telling myself, "One last chance."

I explained to Mr that I had been struggling financially, yet when he heated his man cave, the garage he had converted, he racked up £300 on the heating bill. That was just the beginning. Every time I challenged him about his spending, he got angry. He still owed me money for the house deposit, which he had agreed to pay back but never even tried to.

Despite his promises, he left me to carry 70% of the household bills, and when I asked for help, he said he couldn't, offering no explanation.

I was left confused and angry. Instead, he threw cruel words at me that began to cut deeper: "You're fat," "You smell," "It's all in your head."

One day, in a fit of rage, he sprayed air freshener directly in my face, muttering, "It's your fault."

I was in complete shock and felt as though I was going mad! Mentally, this was such a difficult time in many ways. It got brushed under the carpet, what could I do?!

Then, one day, I stumbled upon a debt collection letter that filled me with a constant sense of anxiety, fearing the debt collectors would knock at the door. It revealed that Mr had accumulated a staggering £2,000 in credit card charges — on gadgets, no less! — which could have gone towards bills instead. He had previously told me he had no money.

Furious, I said, "Leave my bank card on the side, please." "What?" he replied.

"You've been spending money on yourself while I've been struggling to pay the bills," I said.

That was the final straw for him and for me. He exploded in anger, slammed the card on the counter, his face contorted with rage, and stormed out of the door.

THE LAST STRAW

The next morning, on 2nd September 2017, everything escalated. Nile was so sleepy that morning and needed a moment to wake up. As Nile came down the stairs, he climbed onto my lap.

Mr walked past and said, "I'm taking Nile to nursery."

"Okay," I responded.

Mr called Nile, but Nile was tired. Mr stood over us as we were sitting on the sofa, then pulled Nile out of my lap. I heard Nile crying as Mr gripped his teeth. I knew Nile needed a moment, but I also knew that Mr was in a bad mood.

I called out, "Please don't rush him," but he erupted in a fit of rage so intense and full of venom towards me that my heart broke. I tried to shield my little boy from the storm.

I had already been holding my phone, looking at my messages, and I secretly recorded his threats towards me, my hands slightly shaking.

When he turned to my son and said, "Don't worry, son, this is normal," I knew I had to act. This was no environment for a child, and I had to protect Nile. I would not let him grow up in this.

***

So, with the help of a solicitor and a police report, I stood outside the family court in 2018, holding a non-molestation order. That single piece of paper — a lifeline to freedom — promised to keep him out of our home.

I thought I was safe, but the stress continued as he refused to contribute at all to our mortgage or to support Nile. This went on for a year, and he also refused to sell the property. Financially, I sank into considerable debt as I used credit cards to manage my bills, plus to pay for solicitors to help me get court orders.

The cost of freedom was steep. Mr stopped seeing Nile and taking care of him while I worked. Nile missed his dad deeply and kept asking, "When is dad coming?"

I didn't know if or when his dad would reconnect with him due to the spite he had for me. They had a strange yet strong relationship, and I was never going to come between them. I really felt alone.

I didn't have family or friends who could look after Nile so I could return to work. With no support system to rely on, and my mental health deteriorating, I lost my job as a sales manager — a position I had worked years to achieve. I knew that I had lost the ability to work due to being put in this position.

The pressure continued to build when Mr refused to sell the house, knowing full well I could not afford to make the payments alone. I was forced me to sell the house at a loss, plunging me further into debt. I was already late on payments, and my credit cards were maxed out, paying the mortgage and the solicitors to remove Mr from the property.

Days before the exchange of the property, Mr refused to proceed unless he received a certain amount of money, even though we had already agreed he owed me thousands for the deposit I had paid on the house! Eventually, I sold the house at a loss.

I had no choice, and I just wanted peace. I was furious about the amount of money he had stolen from me and Nile, but my desperation to be free from the mental prison far outweighed my anger. I had no choice but to give him the money he asked for due to property law. I could not sell the house without his permission.

What little money I had left came from the remnants of my savings from the sale, which I used to secure a rental. At the end of 2019, I moved in, and it felt like a weight had been lifted off my shoulders.

Generally, Nile and I were happy in the new house, but Nile would often say, "I miss the old house!"

I think moving homes, combined with not seeing his dad, was a lot for a four-year-old. I hoped and believed that I would finally have peace now that I was free from the situation, but the struggles persisted.

I dreaded the thought of justifying my existence at the Job Centre. The shame was suffocating as a woman who had been through an abusive relationship, was jobless, in debt, and had pretty much lost everything in my forties... starting from scratch! Society's judgment of single mothers weighed heavily on me, but I had no choice.

PART IV:
HOMELESSNESS AND AWAKENING

Chapter 10: We Are Homeless

A few months after we moved into our new rented accommodation, I began to enjoy the peace of mind and we settled in. After a few months, I started hearing scratching noises under the floorboards regularly in the evening. My suspicions that it was mice were confirmed when one ran across the living room floor.

The mouse droppings covered my son's bed, and their rotting carcasses filled the walls, creating an unbearable stench. My landlord dismissed my complaints, claiming I was "making it up."

We saw them, both dead and alive, but seeing several mice running across the kitchen surface was another level of horror. I realised the place was infested with mice — their scratching noises haunted us at night.

Despite the many pictures I sent to the landlord, we had to somehow manage with the infestation as finding another property was impossible.

One day, while sitting in the living room, I called my dad (Granddad) for a regular check-in. I wasn't expecting to hear what he was going to say: "You know your dad has been sent to prison."

I looked online… convicted paedophile! How could anyone, let alone my biological father, do such awful things to children? I quickly remembered what my stepmother had told me that day about her daughter! I was glad that he was caught and punished. I often thought about my sisters and wondered how they were, but I had no idea where to start looking for them.

About a month later, my landlord told me she had someone else who wanted the property, knowing my tenancy was about to end. However, I still couldn't find anything I could afford. I was barely managing with the current rent, topping it up using savings.

By then, it was the beginning of the Covid lockdown in 2020. I decided to try to rebuild my life despite my struggles. I had thought about studying to be a barrister for years but was scared to take the leap.

I thought, "I'm not academic! I'm not smart!"

But determined to change Nile's future for the better, I began studying law online. Each completed module was a reminder that I could still dream of something better.

Mother Wounds

My biological mother and I had been communicating regularly, but after Covid, she called me and said she had suffered badly from the virus. I was so glad to hear her voice.

She said, "Don't call asking for him to look after your son," in a firm tone, referring to me asking my stepdad if he could look after my son.

I didn't like the way she said it, implying that I was manipulating my stepdad. She confirmed that was the case.

At that time, I couldn't talk properly as I had to go, it was a short call. I wanted to talk more about it, but we kept missing each other's calls, so I ended up sending her an email expressing exactly how I felt. A couple of times in the past, a therapist had advised me to write a letter to her and burn it, or if I was ready, to give it to my biological mother. But I never did, as I always knew that speaking my truth wasn't acceptable, and it would end in years of silence.

But this was the time... I spoke my truth about how I felt growing up, not feeling like she was there physically enough. I also mentioned how she didn't make an effort to visit me more than a couple of times wherever I lived, and how she never had my son stay overnight once in his seven years of life. I clarified the situation regarding what had happened when I texted my stepdad saying, "If you're having my nephew stay over this weekend, please can you have Nile?"

She was sick at the time and could barely talk. I didn't want to disturb her, so I contacted my stepdad. This was not unusual, as my stepdad had recently contacted me directly regarding another matter on a few occasions.

I felt strongly enough to write that letter because Nile felt the strange relationship between them. I had always felt they didn't have a connection, which was becoming noticeable even to him. Nile had previously said,

"Why can't I stay at grandma's like my cousin, Mum?"

My letter was as diplomatic as I could make it. I didn't think she was intentionally doing anything to hurt me, but when she responded with excuses like, "Your brother needs help, so we have your nephew," I needed help too, but I didn't qualify, I guess...

I realised that nothing would change... In fact, she actually said, "I'm not changing." That was her response!! Along with, "I can't be bothered anymore," referring to our relationship.

I understood that she felt hurt, but I had to speak the truth as I was feeling very uncomfortable. I was tired of holding my tongue and pretending everything was okay, regardless of the consequences.

I tried to bridge the gap in the summer, and she said the month was busy for her birthday. In my mind, I left the ball in her court to reach out when she was ready, as I had other things on my mind.

I started to struggle financially. It was the English saying, "robbing Peter to pay Paul," and as the TV news said, "eating or heating."

My electricity meter was eating money, and I couldn't understand why. Even though I found part-time work at a primary school, food banks became a regular necessity. Then, I faced the unthinkable: a Section 21 (no-fault) eviction notice.

I thought, "What is a Section 21?" It meant that I had done nothing wrong, but the landlord wanted the property back.

For a couple of months, I didn't hear anything more and hoped it had all gone away. But then I received a letter from the local county court confirming that we were going to be evicted. I emailed the local authority (Bexley Council); I needed as much support as possible, especially as someone who had suffered from mental health issues. Unfortunately, I didn't feel they made any reasonable adjustments to support me, despite me sending them a letter from my doctor confirming I had a mental health disability. It seemed like they didn't care... I always felt like "I am just another number."

I called the well-known charities, but their help was limited, and they didn't go into much detail about the homelessness application process for living in temporary accommodation. In my mind, I just thought someone would step in and save Nile and me.

"Of course, they'll help us and give us somewhere to stay." I was nowhere near prepared for the fight with the council that awaited me!

Finally, the day came, 12th September 2022... it was time to be evicted, and luckily it was a school day, so I dropped Nile off at school. I was running around like a headless chicken on my own, trying to pack everything. There was so much stuff, and I had pre-packed as much as I could beforehand.

CHAPTER 11:
EVICTION DAY

The bailiff arrived at 9am. I didn't know what to expect, but he was so calm that he made me feel calm during the ten minutes we spoke. However, when I first saw the landlord in her car, and then ten minutes later, standing at the doorstep while I was still clearing out my belongings, I realised she had arrived early. It made me feel worse, as she watched my every move and obstructed the area I was trying to use to remove my items. I worried about what people would think of me and whether all the neighbours were peering through their curtains, watching me. I had to leave behind my rocking chair, wardrobe, dining room table, chairs, and even the dishwasher. Leaving my belongings behind was frustrating and upsetting, knowing that at some point in the future, I would need them again.

I left my home with two suitcases and made my way to the Bexley council office, as advised by the paperwork the bailiff had given me, to declare myself homeless. Homeless! Wow, I couldn't believe this was happening to me! I had gone from being the woman in elegant dresses at cocktail parties in lavish hotels to carrying everything I owned in two suitcases.

Arriving at the council office at 9.30am, I encountered the unwelcoming assistant who asked me to fill out the forms. I felt like I was waiting for ages, sitting and watching all the people coming in and going out, waiting to be called and given a place to stay. Two hours passed before I was told to go, and that someone would call me.

I thought, "Go where?" I didn't have anywhere to go.

I took my belongings and began to walk. I found myself sitting in a coffee shop, anxiously waiting until it was time for the school run.

I picked up Nile from school, and as I greeted him with a hug, he said, "Where are we going?" eyeing the bags in my hands.

I replied, "I don't know, but let's go to the park."

I sat on the park bench, impatiently waiting while watching my eight-year-old son run around with not a care in the world. Truthfully, I was stalling him at the park because we had nowhere to go. Then, THE call came in at 4.30pm. It was the council, saying we were being placed in shared temporary accommodation.

Those words—"SHARED, TEMPORARY, ACCOMMODATION"— scared the life out of me.

I broke down in tears and begged them to let us be placed somewhere that wasn't shared. It was a massive trigger for my mental health, especially after being in an abusive relationship. We were very vulnerable and sensitive to noise and people in general.

The staff member on the phone said, "I understand it's hard."

I was furious. I responded, "Have YOU been through this before?"

She said, "No."

I snapped back, "Then how can you understand?"

She then said, "Accept the offer, there is no other option!"

At this point, I knew we had nowhere to go, and I accepted. We made our way to the address.

The building looked like a glorified prison. It was on a steep hill and used to be a care home for the elderly. The building had four floors and housed approximately 50 other families.

After we checked in with the building manager, who greeted us with a smile on her face, she said, "Don't make trouble, as it doesn't get you a place quicker!"

I didn't really understand what she meant; I was so overwhelmed by everything happening in that moment. The paperwork the manager gave me said the council had 56 days to make a decision on our application and, if accepted, they had a duty to house us. The countdown had begun.

As we were escorted through the building, the several heavy doors banged loudly behind us. It felt like forever to reach our room because I had so many heavy bags, and the lift wasn't working, so we had to climb the stairs. The staff member told us that one of the shower rooms wasn't working before she led us to a double room that was to be our space — two single beds, a sink, and a small fridge freezer with a built-in wardrobe. You could see the disappointment in my son's face.

I turned to him and said, "It's not forever! It's just somewhere to stay until we get our own place."

The walls were thin, the facilities broken, and the strangers felt like threats. The shared kitchen was a battlefield of filth, and the bathrooms were breeding grounds for despair. I think I was so tired and in shock that I couldn't fully comprehend what had happened.

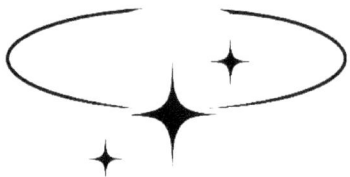

Chapter 12:
Fight for Our Rights

A couple of weeks later, I realised what the building manager meant when she said, "Don't make trouble" when we checked in. "Trouble" meant complaining. There were issues with the building, such as the radiator not working in the shower room, fire alarms going off at night, noisy neighbours, and it felt like we just had to put up with it.

I watched my son grow anxious and clingy, unable to sleep, frightened by the banging doors and late-night arguments. At night, as he slept, I cried silently, praying for a miracle.

I felt ashamed, embarrassed, humiliated, and worthless living in that accommodation. In the next few months, my mind wandered. I felt like I was in limbo, exposed.

My housing case was passed from person to person within the housing team, who all asked the same questions and required the same information.

On one occasion, I did not hear from my caseworker for a month, so I contacted the housing department manager at the council, who said, "It takes as long as it takes."

Was I being unreasonable, or did I deserve this?!

I began questioning myself and started to believe what they were telling me—that it was "my fault."

The accommodation was home to many different types of people—families, but also single people. Sometimes there were drug addicts; I could smell drugs in the hallway. There were psychotic mental health patients and loud arguments between people living on-site. Groups of girls would hang around the communal areas, which could be quite intimidating, especially when they sat on kitchen countertops while I was washing up. I just kept to myself and avoided people, which was isolating at times.

Sharing the bathrooms and kitchen was unhygienic. I cleaned the cooker hood and found 20 flies stuck to it with grease. I often avoided cooking because I had to clean the kitchen thoroughly before making a meal, so I ended up buying takeaways. I frequently had to clean the toilets as others would leave sanitary towels or faeces around. These conditions felt unbearable.

I spoke to my doctor constantly because I thought I was losing my mind, as the antidepressants were not enough. She referred me to a psychiatrist. It felt like a lifetime before I received an appointment with the NHS psychiatrist at the mental health centre. I walked into the mental health centre feeling very anxious about what they would say. I was scared they might section me, and it didn't help when I saw other patients in the hot waiting room looking suspicious.

The psychiatrist called my name: "Shantel Morris." He guided me to his room, where another person was already present.

The doctor said, "This is a student who will be sitting in with us," and the in-depth personal questioning began.

Eventually, he diagnosed me with bipolar disorder. I had known I was different my whole life and had always struggled with my mental health, but in this homeless situation, it was becoming dangerous. My mind was so overwhelmed that I recently accidentally poured boiling water over my hand, thinking I was turning the tap on while Nile asked me for help as I made a cup of tea. I thought I was going mad, that it was all in my head. But this diagnosis helped me, and the psychiatrist prescribed me mood stabilisers and talking therapies. I knew, deep down, I could only get better in an environment where I felt safe. I needed to do more.

Constantly hiding my feelings, as I had to be strong in front of my son, was draining.

After three months, Nile started asking, "Have you heard from the council yet?" But the hardest part was when other families were housed before us, even though they had spent less time in the accommodation.

I would reluctantly tell Nile that they were leaving, as he would see them go, and you could see his heart drop every time before he would burst into tears and cry, "When are we going, Mum?" This broke my heart!

The walls were so thin that Nile could hear my neighbour's inappropriate conversations in the evening as he tried to sleep. I saw how living (if you could call it that!) in the accommodation was beginning to seriously affect my son. Nile started to have severe anxiety issues and OCD behaviours. My son was terrified to go to the toilet alone, or if I left the room without him, to use the toilet. We were unable to sleep because of the banging doors and hearing noises all night long. While my son slept, I cried and prayed, eventually falling asleep but always keeping one eye open, ready in case something happened in the building.

Nile's development took a step back. He had been used to sleeping in his own room before the eviction and felt safe in his own home, which built his confidence, but that changed in shared housing. Nile and I were unable to sleep peacefully and had become shells of ourselves. Nile became even more clingy. I took him to the doctor and school because I knew he needed support; the school referred him to children's mental health services. Finally, some support was coming through for us. Maybe the tides were turning for me and my son.

This hope was dashed when the first decision letter came from the council after eight months, not the 56 days as stated on the paperwork. The letter said I had made myself intentionally homeless.

The council claimed I had arrears and made myself homeless, but I couldn't understand this decision, as it was a no-fault eviction, not an arrears eviction. At this point, I knew I needed help. There were some arrears because I had struggled with my mental health during Covid, and I had started buying things I didn't need, gambling, etc. However, this was confirmed by my psychiatrist as a symptom of bipolar disorder, a mental health disability I didn't know I had at the time of my actions. The psychiatrist said I was not under the correct care or medication, I had been triggered into mania, which causes uncontrollable spending and gambling with risky behaviours.

I knew I could not give up because Nile needed me to live and fight for him. He didn't deserve this, [I didn't deserve this]! I found an exceptional professional legal aid solicitor at GT Stewart who fought the council on my behalf. This enabled me to focus on Nile and my mental health. My solicitor immediately noticed that the council had used the wrong procedure to complete the first decision of intentional homelessness and requested that I be reassessed.

Social services came to see us and spoke to Nile's teachers at school, asking many questions regarding my ability to look after him. I was terrified they would take my son. I had suicidal thoughts, but I knew that my son was relying on me, and if I wasn't there for him, he would have been devastated and traumatised further.

Six weeks later, Bexley council responded to my appeal, saying that I was intentionally homeless again (my fault) and that I didn't have a mental health disability with bipolar disorder, even though I had provided several medical documents confirming I did. This entire experience was so frustrating because they refused to listen to medical advice, even from their own doctors.

Just when I thought it couldn't get any worse, my solicitor told me the council was moving families to areas in the north of England, four hours away from where we lived. I was terrified! How would my son manage being moved away from everything he knew on top of everything else he'd been through?

On two occasions, the council was about to evict Nile and I, which would literally have meant we would have been put out on the street because of the decisions they made. I felt like I was losing my mind with stress and exhaustion. I needed a miracle!

This is when the feelings of guilt hit... Had I put my son through this terrible situation? I was hopeless. Then a wave of anger washed over me as tears streamed down my face. These tears transformed into strength. I felt a force of energy within me, giving me strength I had never had before.

I said, "Come on, Shantel!"

Something shifted — while I couldn't change the external, I could change the internal... me. This was it... MY POWER. I had had enough of crying and being treated this way! I had to fight for my son's life and mine like never before. I needed to be seen and heard. I was not going to allow my son to suffer more than he already had.

But my true fight was about changing my mindset, and as my mindset changed, my faith grew. I focused on finding peace within myself, happiness within. I prayed more and meditated. I begged God to help me in any way possible and tried to be grateful for what I did have, remembering that at least Nile was with me. My son and I regularly listened to frequency and angelic music to help us sleep. I focused on my law studies and spent time in nature, trying to keep myself busy and staying out of the accommodation as much as I could. My part-time job with the kids at the primary school was also a good distraction. I had "me time" at the gym, laughed with my friends, and went to the seaside on occasion for a change of scenery.

I would tell my granddad and aunty the crazy incidents at the accommodation, and I had to find the humour in them, or I would have cried. Laughter really helped. My uncle and two cousins checked in on me, and there were amazing people I met in the accommodation who reminded me who I was, with no judgement. They made Nile and I feel like humans and not numbers!

After speaking to several families in the accommodation, I realised that they needed help too and started to share my experiences with tips to help them through. Helping others also gave me hope. I started to see these families leave and move to new places after helping them. It was so fulfilling seeing the transformation of a parent knowing they were leaving.

I had so much faith in my government-funded solicitor (GT Stewart). Chris Morris was relentless in chasing Bexley council and kept me updated constantly while he planned to take the council to court. We're still waiting for the third appeal decision response from the council. Finally, after nearly a year, the council offered us private accommodation. It wasn't just a home; it was hope.

After I accepted the private accommodation, the council sent the final appeal decision, confirming that I did have a mental disability but was no longer homeless because I had been offered a property. The Housing Ombudsman told the council to formally apologise to me and compensate me for not helping me before I was evicted to store my belongings.

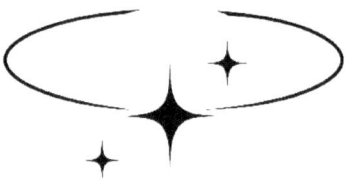

Chapter 13: Follow the Yellow Brick Road

God sent me the right people at the right time, the opportunities to help me, and the strength to sustain me. This experience taught me to believe in myself. I believe God wants me to share my story to help others find their way. Most of the battle is in your mind.

Start changing your mindset to: "I can do this" and just do it. Look after yourself—what you consume, who you surround yourself with, and your environment all play a part in shaping your mindset.

It is clear to me that by changing my mindset, and healing myself from within, staying positive, and taking positive action, things in my life would start to turn in my favour. Despite all the turmoil, I completed my law diploma, and I am due to finish my law degree in the summer of 2026. I want to use my degree to help others. I have completed legal housing training with Shelter (homeless charity).

After everything I've been through, God confirmed what I had been feeling deep within. He gave me a vision: to write a book about my life and reveal my true purpose. That purpose is now unfolding. Part of it is to help others through the non-profit I founded, **Morris Mission** (www.morrismission.com)

Morris Mission runs workshops for vulnerable families facing eviction and those living in temporary accommodation. It's a message of hope. We also support housing professionals with tools and training to better serve vulnerable members of the community.

My first Morris Mission workshop was a coffee morning for survivors of domestic abuse. One of the women said she didn't even know she had to apply to the council when she was in the refuge. Another woman said that the workshop was very informative and delivered perfectly.

This workshop reminded me that many families are homeless due to domestic abuse, and how necessary Morris Mission is in supporting them to understand the housing system after being placed in refuges.

These workshops provide critical support at the exact moment families need it most. Morris Mission hopes to work with Prince William, as he is a champion for preventing homelessness in the UK. I am also actively seeking funding from the government, philanthropists, corporate businesses, and anyone moved to support this work, to help grow the organisation.

Free Morris Mission workshops should be mandatory across the nation, providing basic access to justice, which is a human right under the Human Rights Act 1998. This could easily be added to housing legislation as an amendment to the Housing Act 2004 or the Homelessness Reduction Act 2017.

Morris Mission has been awarded funding from the National Lottery Awards for All, which is a great achievement and shows that they believe in Morris Mission and want to support vulnerable families facing homelessness. Additionally, most local ward councillors in the area are on board with Morris Mission and are actively promoting us.

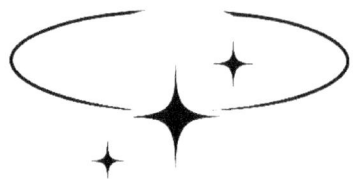

Epilogue: I Once Was Lost But Now I Am Found

I've come to accept that, for the first time, I have chosen myself. I can truly say: **I love myself**. I no longer neglect my needs for the sake of others. I am now my biggest supporter; I make time for myself to meditate or simply take a mindful walk.

What I was missing all along was love—the love I needed to give to my inner child and the self-love I had to rediscover as an adult. That love is now the foundation of everything I do. It is my destiny to continue growing into the best version of myself and to help others find their way back to themselves, too.

They say that "home is where the heart is." Home is not just a place. To truly find home is to remember who you are and why you are here—your soul's purpose.

Life will always ask you to take risks. If you deeply believe in something, don't wait for the fear to disappear—it won't. Courage doesn't mean being fearless; it means acting in spite of fear. Balance is the key to life!

If there's one lesson I carry with me, it's this: **Believe in yourself**. You are worthy. You deserve love. Don't let anyone walk over you—you are far stronger than you realise. We all have a purpose, but we also have free will. We can choose to remain lost, or we can choose to be found.

My journey is proof of the power of hope, faith, and charity. It's taught me to believe in myself and trust that, even in the darkest times, a purpose is waiting to be fulfilled. If my story inspires even one person to keep going, then every tear, every sleepless night, and every prayer will have been worth it.

Today, my son Nile and I are secure, stable, and grateful. Nile now has support for what we now know is neurodiversity, which can be challenging at times. However, there is a team of people working with Nile to support him, and he will be starting secondary school next year — and our journey continues.

According to Shelter's August 2024 report, **151,000 children in the UK are homeless and living in temporary accommodation**. If you would like to support or donate to help these families, please visit morrismission.com (Registered Community Interest Company: **16308743**).

www.ingramcontent.com/pod-product-compliance
Lightning Source LLC
Chambersburg PA
CBHW061225070526
44584CB00029B/3991